Where the Past Lives
—Constellation Road

by

Dana W. Burden

and

Joe Stevens

Copyright notice

Copyright© 2006 by Dana W. Burden Joe Stevens. All rights reserved. Printed in the United States of America. Except as permitted under the United States Copyright Act of 1976, no part of this publication may be reproduced or distributed in any form or by any means, or stored in a database or retrieval system, without the prior written permission of Dana W. Burden or Joe Stevens. Notwithstanding the above sentence, permission is hereby granted for journalists to quote brief passages for use in newspapers, periodicals or broadcasts, provided full prominent credit is given to *Where the Past Lives—Constellation Road* by Dana W. Burden and Joe Stevens.

Library of Congress Control Number: 2006900118
IBSN: 0-9765591-1-0
Pathfinder Publishing, P.O. Box 1494, Wickenburg, Arizona

Table of Contents

Table of Contents	iii
Dedication	v
Foreword	vi
Preface	vii
About the authors	xi
Mining terminology	xiii

Leaving Wickenburg and Heading Out 1

King Solomon Wash and Sayers Station 13

$17,000 Highway and the Unida Group 17

The Monte Cristo 27

The Black Rock 37

More Sights Along the $17,000 Highway 39

The Gold Bar 45

End of the Line—The Williams Ranch 53

Postface	57
Appendix: Rich Hill	59
References	63
Index	65

Acknowledgements:

Without the help of Jim Liggett this book would simply not exist. He has spent countless hours using his software to format this book, enter the pictures and make this book happen. We are deeply obligated to him.

There were others who provided wonderful assistance and contributions. Specifically thanks to proofers Ed Romanski, Pete Peterson, Stan Watson and MaryAnn Igna of the Desert Caballeros Western Museum. Once again, Jim Liggett was an exceptional help in this effort.

We could not have done without the help of Jack and Laura Culp for details on Rich Hill, the Wickenburg Desert Caballeros Western Museum for many folders of interest and the Sharlott Hall Museum in Prescott for use of their excellent files of newspapers from the late 1800's and early 1900's. Additionally, the folks at the Arizona Department of Mines and Mineral Resources were wonderful pulling files, talking with us about our research and providing details.

Thanks to all!

Dedication

It may seem odd to dedicate this book to one of its authors, nevertheless, so it will be!

I, author Joe Stevens, dedicate this book to my co-author, cohort, and very special friend, Dana Burden. As he points out in the Forward, Dana has wanted to produce a book anyone could use to learn about our desert and specifically *Where the Past Lives—Constellation Road*.

Dana has not only been an inspiration for this book but also has worked long and hard for the betterment of our Wickenburg community and of the surrounding desert.

It is his love of Arizona, his upbeat manner, his love of storytelling, and more specifically, his love of the Sonoran Desert around Wickenburg, that has educated thousands upon thousands about the Wickenburg area and Arizona. His recognition by the Arizona Historical Foundation as an Arizona Culture Keeper attests to his dedication.

Dana is a special gem. Thanks for making me a part of Wickenburg Jeep Tours and all the learning and fun we have had. Thanks also for all the wonderful hikes and trips including Hunts Mesa, South of Monument Valley and our hike into the Grand Canyon.

Joe Stevens

Foreword

This little book is a labor of love for Joe and Dana. Dana's affair with this wonderful road began in the 1940s, after WWII, when the Remuda Ranch had four-wheel-drive jeeps that allowed them back onto long-abandoned mine roads. At the Remuda Ranch, Dana and family entertained their guests with pack trips along the area's trails and with and 4x4 rides. When Joe moved here, Dana had just started Wickenburg Jeep Tours. Several of their tours were taken along Constellation Road. We loved introducing visitors to the wonders of the Sonoran Desert and the mining history. For the past three years we have led highly acclaimed mine history tours for the Desert Caballeros Western Museum. Writing the book *Desert Hiking Out Wickenburg Way* got Dana and Joe out along the road dozens of times. We thought there ought to be some way to get people out there more simply and a guide book came to mind. Also as historians, we wanted to highlight the importance of this road in the early history of Arizona. Doing the research has been eye opening; note the story of Rich Hill and the in-depth studies of the actual mines (Joe's area of expertise). Putting it together meant many wonderful hours measuring, photographing and enjoying. Also treasured were visits with Roy and Carrol Williams at their very special Williams Family Guest Ranch. This pristine country is so beautiful and easily accessible with an adequate road that we hope you'll give it one or several tries. Just the view from Mahoney Ridge is worth your effort.

Preface

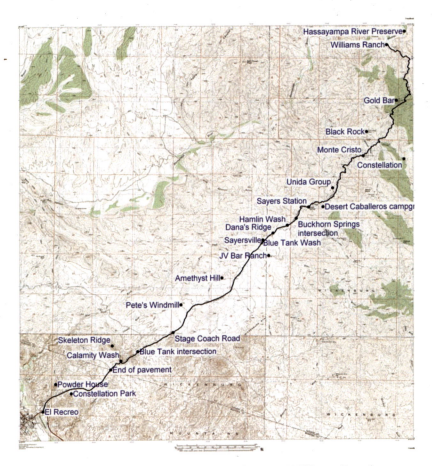

Constellation Road from Wickenburg to Williams Ranch

HOW TO USE THIS BOOK.

While Dana has authored a hiking book, neither of us are English majors nor what would normally be thought of as an "author." Rather, we are both "story tellers." You will find this book written as a story of Constellation Road and what you can see at along each step of the way. A "narrated history" if you will.

Our goal is for you to be able to drive along the road and learn at least some of its rich history. Routinely, we take folks on tour who have lived here for years and driven the road many times. The primary words we hear are: "I didn't know that!" or "I've never seen that before!"

Here is your chance to "know it and see it" all by yourself. Drive safely and thoroughly enjoy your story tellers' tales.

TRIP PREPARATION:

Do NOT make this trip if there is any chance for rain in these mountains north and east of Wickenburg. You must traverse several normally dry streams and drive in stream bottoms. Flash flooding can happen very quickly and leave you either stranded or worse!

Be sure to allow yourself at least 5 hours to make the round trip, including the stops along the way. Going only one way, with no stops, it takes about one hour to get to or return from the Williams Ranch.

Mine areas: Do not enter any mine tunnel. Cave-ins are more frequent when the area is disturbed. Additionally, be very careful around the entrance of any vertical or incline shaft. Some will have a concrete collar around the top of the shaft. These collars are not normally very deep into the ground, hence water can wash out around them making sink holes that drop directly into the shaft. Use good judgment, enjoy the sights but stay safe.

Vehicle: Take along the following items at the minimum:

Tow strap, shovel, jumper cables, first aid kit, water for the vehicle and a cell phone. A heavy duty jack can also be very helpful. Be sure your vehicle is in good mechanical shape and that all fluid levels are full—especially the gas! We recommend only a high clearance vehicle and prefer it to be four wheel drive. However, a two-wheel-drive vehicle can normally negotiate this road. There are many sand washes and very rough spots that you will need to traverse. This is not a road for the uninitiated desert driver. For those of us who routinely do this kind of thing, it still requires our constant attention. Don't push yourself if you are unsure. Instead see the educational curator at the Desert Caballeros Western Museum and schedule yourself for one of their tours along this route.

Personal: Be sure you take plenty of water for this trip. One gallon per person would be too little if you had to walk out some 16 miles. It is also a good idea to take along some snacks or even a picnic lunch. Use hydrolytes and hi-energy bars as well. Be sure the individual who has the cell phone has on a good pair of hiking shoes. You may have to climb to the top of a hill to receive cell phone service. Actually, each person should have on good hiking shoes. This is no place for flip flops!

CRITTERS:

The desert is home to many wonderful animals, however, some should be avoided. Do NOT play with rattlesnakes! Rattlesnakes are not the hazard of common folklore. In Arizona about one person dies of rattlesnake bite every two years, and almost always these unfortunates have been trying to handle a snake. The snake will be very happy if you do not disturb them so they can get out of your way. There is no reason to kill them. The desert is where they live and they are a part of the balance of nature. If anyone is bitten by a rattlesnake, get the person into the vehicle and keep them as calm as possible. Depart immediately and go directly to the Wickenburg Hospital Emergency Room.

Beware of scorpions. We rarely see them. If you turn over a rock however, you may be surprised. They will quickly scurry away. Scorpion stings are very painful but not usually life threatening except to the very young.

Gila Monsters are rarely seen and protected by the State. They are beautiful to see and will continue to move away from you. Do not chase them or prod them; they too are poisonous. They are a part of nature in our wonderful desert.

Deer, coyotes, mountain lions, bob cats and javelina are all potential sights you may encounter. They are all much faster than you!

FENCES:

If you depart Constellation Road for any side trip you may encounter fences and gates. If you go through a gate that is closed, reclose it. If you go through a gate that is open, leave it open.

DISCLAIMER:

The authors, publishers and all those associated with this book, directly or indirectly, disclaim any liability for accidents, injury, damages or loses that may occur to anyone using this book. The responsibility for good health and safety while riding or hiking is that of the user.

About the authors

DANA BURDEN is a native of Wickenburg having been reared on the Remuda Guest Ranch. He has "kicked the dust" of most every horse or hiking trail in the Wickenburg area, many throughout the state and Southwest, and several in Mexico and Australia. Dana was a Grand Canyon river boat certified guide. He has led numerous horseback rides through Monument Valley and in the Flagstaff area. He also led the Desert Caballeros cowboy ride for many years through the Weaver and Bradshaw mountains north of Wickenburg. He is a founding member of Wickenburg Clean and Beautiful, a group whose charter not only calls for keeping the desert clean, but also for building hiking and horseback trails around Wickenburg. Dana started Wickenburg Jeep Tours and was instrumental in educating thousands of folks about the Wickenburg area and the desert.

On April 30th, 2004, Dana was honored as an "Arizona Culture Keeper." This title was bestowed by the Arizona Historical Foundation and honors individuals as the "...existing pioneers of our state because of entrepreneurial spirit, business or civic leadership, or passionate contributions to the cause that is distinctly Arizona."

JOE STEVENS was born in Ironwood, Michigan and lived his first 18 years in Montreal, Wisconsin. He grew up in this iron mining community where his father worked as the safety engineer in the deepest underground iron-ore mine in the world. He spent his days along the mine dumps and, with his father, frequently visited all the buildings and equipment associated with this huge mining operation. He spent his career as an officer in the United States Air Force specializing in the field of intelligence—piecing data together to know about the bad guy!

Upon arrival in Wickenburg and his association with Dana in the jeep tour business, he put his investigative skills and his knowledge of mining to good use. He quickly learned that you cannot take folks on a jeep tour and let them start talking. They will take over the tour so you better have plenty to tell them. His love for the desert, all the wonderful mining history and the joy of educating folks made that an easy job and this book a "natural."

Joe is a docent at the Desert Caballeros Western Museum in Wickenburg and each spring leads tours along Constellation Road as well as to other ghost town areas.

Mining terminology

Before we get into the portion of this book where we witness several mines, let's take the opportunity to understand some basic terminology connected with all mines. You will probably want to refer back to this section.

HEADFRAME: The wooden or metal framework structure that sits over the entrance to the shaft. It is important to a mine as it supports the big pulley for the skip and cage that move people, supplies and ore up and down the shaft.

SHAFT: The vertical or inclined tunnel used to enter/exit the mine and through which all supplies/miners enter and all minerals, waste rock and miners exit.

LEVEL: A term to describe all of the tunnels at a given elevation down in the shaft. In most mines there is a level every 100 vertical feet.

DRIFT: A horizontal tunnel from the shaft outward. Normally a drift does not exit the mountain (see adit).

CROSSCUT: A horizontal tunnel 90 degrees to a drift.

STOPE: Miners drill and blast upward from a drift or crosscut. As the materials fall they are "mucked" into an ore car and taken out. The resulting big hole above the level is a stope (big room).

ADIT: A horizontal tunnel from the shaft outward to the side of the mountain drilled through non-ore-bearing rock. It's purpose is to promote air circulation as well as laying track to move ore and waste rock from the mine without having to lift it all the way to the head frame.

SKIP: Those enclosures that either carry materials into the mine or ore and waste rock out. A skip is attached to the hoist engine cable that runs over the head frame pulley and is, in essence, an elevator.

CAGE: The enclosure that carries men into and out of the mine. Again, it is attached to the hoist engine cable that runs over the head frame pulley and is an elevator.

COLLAR: The neck of the shaft at the surface. This area may be constructed of wood (possibly now rotten) or concrete.

STAMP MILL: A machine that crushes ore using piston-like devices.

FRUE VANNER: A machine for concentrating ore, used for separating gold as it comes off the stamp batteries.

WILFLEY TABLE: An inclined percussion table, usually with longitudinal grooves in its surface, vibrated by side blows at right angles to the flow of a slurry mixture. It was developed in 1896 and named after its inventor.

Mining terminology

Chapter 1: Leaving Wickenburg and Heading Out

Hitch up the wagon, don your toughest Levis then head east on the "highway" that began the migration into Central Arizona.

The Highway started in downtown Wickenburg, right off today's Wickenburg Way main street. To get to it today, you go east of the Hassayampa River bridge two blocks and take El Recreo to the north. (As you turn off highway 60 on to El Recreo, set your trip odometer at mileage 0.0; see map in Preface, p. vii) In the old days, the population gathered at mine sites in the Weaver and Bradshaw Mountains. The current road down the river toward Phoenix did not exist. If travelers needed to head south to the Pima settlements or on to Tucson, they went east on Constellation then south on what is now called the Stagecoach Road. It actually connected Wickenburg to the booming settlements of San Domingo and Little San Domingo washes. El Recreo dead ends and to the right Constellation heads east up Powder House

Powder House Wash with high school "W" on top of hill

Wash. Where was the powder house (mileage 0.4)? The powder house is up the wash on the right side of this peak, located on private property. The road passes Constellation Park, site of the Town of Wickenburg rodeo grounds (mileage 0.8). We continue

Constellation Park

on east past the site of Jack Burden's (Dana's dad) infamous Lion Hunt in the 1930s. Jack was always looking for ways to promote Wickenburg and to entertain Remuda Guest Ranch clients. A fellow showed up claiming to have captured a wild mountain lion. He had dogs and offered a real lion hunt. Each hunter paid X dollars then more bucks into a pool to go to the one who shot the lion. The day arrived, the town folks gathered, and hunters mounted their best rough-country horses or mules. The promoter let the lion out of the cage and it headed for the hills. After reasonable lead time he let the howling dogs out to track the lion. More time passed, then the hunters were turned loose to scatter and crash through the brush trying to find a way over or around Skeleton Ridge where Mr. Lion had disappeared. After a while the well-trained lion streaked back to the truck and jumped into his cage followed shortly by the hounds, the promoter jumped into the truck and headed out and away with the money, leaving everyone suckered.

We drive on to Skeleton Ridge on your left front just across the

View of Skeleton Ridge from Constellation Road

county line into Yavapai County where the pavement ends. Skeleton Ridge got its name in the 1930s when the skeleton of a redheaded woman was found in a cave on the ridge. Old newspapers related that in the late 1800s a man and wife at Constellation fought so hard she left for Wickenburg never to be seen again. What happened to her remains a mystery? Did Indians or bad men do her in or did dehydration drive her to the cave for shade. Is the skeleton really that of the woman?

At the county line (mileage 2.1) see a gate on right. You can park and walk through this gate, follow the directions in *Desert Hiking Out Wickenburg Way* to visit Three Falls, a nifty rock formation and a really pretty area when the stream is running clear water. Stay away when flooded with muddy water!

You drive forward into Calamity Wash (mileage 2.4). The

Approaching Calamity Wash on Constellation Road

unusual name comes from the Constellation area miners desire to celebrate the 4th of July back before the turn of the century. They pooled money and sent a man to Wickenburg to acquire a barrel of whiskey. He, of course, had to sample all available and a few at the bar. He headed back with the barrel in the back of the buckboard, went around this sharp corner in the wash too fast. The barrel rolled out and split open. That was a great Calamity! This story is actually a fabrication of Dana's mother,

Sophie Burden, who loved to spin yarns for the ranch guests. It's a great story, isn't it? Nevertheless, it is still called Calamity today. Walk a short ways up this wash to see a cave with smoke black on the ceiling from the ancient Indians. Further up the left fork of this wash there are petroglyphs on the rocks.

Petroglyphs in Calamity Wash

Driving on one-half mile, we pass the turn off now called Blue Tank Road (mileage 3.0). The road to the right goes to the

Constellation-Blue Tank Road intersection

former headquarters of the 10X Ranch. This ranch stretches all the way to San Domingo Wash, some 8 miles south of town and was founded by the Macias family, still prominent in the area. Blue Tank Road goes cross country to Rincon Road on the Hassayampa River. This is the way to town for residents of Rincon when the Hassayampa River is too high to cross. It also leads to several excellent trail heads for hikers and riders.

You now meander through beautiful Sonoran Desert to the junction with the Stagecoach Road (mileage 4.0). This rugged but 4x4-passable road connects to the Castle Hot Springs Road some 12 miles south. Along its route you pass the side roads to long abandoned The Great Southern, Tindale, Purple Passion, and Monarch mines and many unnamed prospects. It crosses San

Intersection of the Stagecoach Road

Domingo Wash, which hosted many more mines, mills and the Sanger Dam.

The next road to the left goes to Pete's Windmill (mileage 4.6)

Pete's Windmill (Rich Hill in background)

named for Pete Fletcher of Remuda Ranch, who for many years ranched the Rincon Ranch. This windmill is a major water source for many of the popular trail rides enjoying this area. The road extends on into Blue Tank Wash. On the ridge before the wash was the "Goat Camp," a popular picnic and camping site. Continuing, you now drive over a red clay hill where shortly you will note a road on the left (mileage 5.3) that goes behind a hill (Amethyst) and down a wash past an old home site, now a big corral and windmill. This old road was a wagon road into Blue Tank Wash, thence on to cross the Hassayampa to a stage stop, where Dana lived in as a kid. Dana claims growing up with a few ghosts was standard for the day. His favorite was one that came in through the screen door, walked down the hall and into the middle room, then sat down and shuffled cards. Sadly photos of this historic site were lost when the Desert Caballeros Western Museum burned in '73. The old road probably served the mines before the present road was constructed. At six miles Constellation Road crosses a cattle guard (mileage 5.9); this fence separates the Rincon Ranch from JV Bar Ranch. On your left is Amethyst Hill where you can crack open rocks and, if lucky, might find a gem.

Amethyst Hill

Along this stretch of road, any side road goes to old prospects, shafts, tunnels and other very dangerous remains of mining efforts; be careful while enjoying the beautiful rocks. At the next junction (mileage 7.2), the road to the right goes to the headquarters of the JV Bar Ranch. This huge ranch takes in over 100 sec-

Entrance to the JV Bar Ranch

tions (640 acres per section, a square mile) going over Denver Hill into Buckhorn Wash. Check your odometer reading at this point. Readings can vary so correct your mileage to that provided.

Moving forward you now drop into Blue Tank Wash. Look to the left on a rise beyond the wash (mileage 7.4) for the site of Sayersville. A Mr. Sayers is said to have built a store and post office here; it also boasted a school. We think it was established in one of those wet years when Blue Tank Wash appeared to have permanent flow. When the wash dried up, he moved to the spring in King Solomons Wash, the present site of Sayers Station. Proceeding on we cross Dana's Ridge (mileage 7.5), so named when Dana Burden brought many groups here to camp for three-day trail rides. Continue on and you drive into Hamlin Wash (mileage 7.8), which downstream shortly runs into King Solomons Wash.

For an interesting side trip requiring a 4x4 vehicle, see the chapter on Vulcan City in *Desert Hiking Out Wickenburg Way*. You

View as Constellation Road drops into Blue Tank Wash

View of Dana's Ridge just past JV Bar entrance

Hamlin wash—normally dry

can visit Camp B mine and with a half-mile walk (or a very tough drive in a 4x4) visit Vulcan City.

On Constellation Road proceed forward to a major junction (mileage 8.5). Right is the Buckhorn Springs Road on to Castle Hot Springs and Lake Pleasant; straight is Constellation Road into King Solomon Wash.

After passing the Buckhorn Springs Road, look off to your left to the west-north-west. You will see the Weaver Mountains. In the foreground is a peak called Sam Powell Peak. The predominant peak in the Weavers, which sits forward of the rest, is called Rich Hill. Surrounding this peak is the area that "started it all" for the Wickenburg area. See Appendix I for the detail.

Constellation Road straight ahead, Buckhorn Road to right

Sam Powell Peak is in the foreground with Rich Hill to the left and behind in the Weaver Mountains

Chapter 2: King Solomon Wash and Sayers Station

(We sometimes save this stop for the return trip as it provides a nice break.)

Moving ahead, as you enter King Solomon wash you will see a windmill on your right (mileage 8.8). If you went left downstream there are antique roads (4x4) going to the Hassayampa, the White Mine and the tallest saguaro. Turn right and head upstream to Sayers Station,,

Tallest saguaro at 50 feet 6 inches

tucked in the trees on the right side (mileage 9.1). Dana remembers when the station had a two story house with a rock bottom and frame top. It was the bar, bawdy house, café, market and post office. Be sure to check the water spigot at the concrete steps, then follow the trail up hill to the cave from which the water comes. Further upstream on King Solomon Wash is an excellent camp site used by horse groups, hikers

Sayers Station—steps with water spigot on right

Sayers Station—all that remains of the community

and ATV groups (see next chapter). There are also several mines, many prospects and spectacular old trails.

Sayers Station—desert springs occur in the strangest places.

Chapter 3: $17,000 Highway and the Unida Group

Across the wash from Sayers Station, Constellation Road now goes uphill on a sometimes well maintained road (mileage 9.1). This road

Entrance to $17000 highway just across wash from Sayers Station

between Sayers Station and the Gold Bar Mine is the famous $17,000 highway. In 1877 James Mahoney discovered gold and named the site the Gold Bar Mine. He needed a better wagon road than the existing stage road over which to get his ore to market. In 1893 he and four men (between January and August) built this passable wagon road between Sayers and his Gold Bar claims. Mahoney claimed it connected the Black Rock Mining District with an older wagon road between Phoenix and Prescott via Castle Creek. With 4x4s and knowledge of which trails to take, you can still make this journey today.

As you climb this hill, notice the construction at the curves. The rock work on downhill side is exceptional and in most cases has not washed out in over 100 years—quite an engineering feat.

Continuing uphill note the beautiful view to the right down into the large camping area upstream from Sayers Station. For 58 years this

Desert Caballeros camp site

location was used by the Desert Caballeros horseback ride as either the first night's stop on the way out of town or the last night's stop on the way back. Imagine six camps with 250 men, over 250 horses/mules, mess area, etc. all in this space. Many riders agree that it was the best camp site of them all.

As you top the first ridge look left to the ruins of the Unida Group of mines (mileage 9.9). A 107 acre parcel was purchased in 2004. Will it be reopened as a mine or developed as home sites?

View from Constellation Road into the Unida Mine group with incline shaft center right and vertical shaft at the tailing pile (stop less than one-tenth mile from top of hill)

This area has several shafts, collectively called the Unida Group. The actual start of the mining operation is unknown; however, based on some of the old rock houses in the area, mining probably began in the 1870s or 1880s. Just one-tenth mile after topping the hill and looking over the area, look down to your left and note these old rock buildings. There are also remnants of several other buildings in the area, all of which used concrete and mortar and are of more recent construction. These were probably built in the early 1900s. The old hotel site, a flat dirt site today, only has a set of concrete steps leading up to what was the wooden hotel building.

In 1918 this area, formerly known as the United Mining Co. and then known as the Arizona Copper and Gold Co., became the Unida Group. The total area of 12 claims was 208¾ acres. Within the area there are

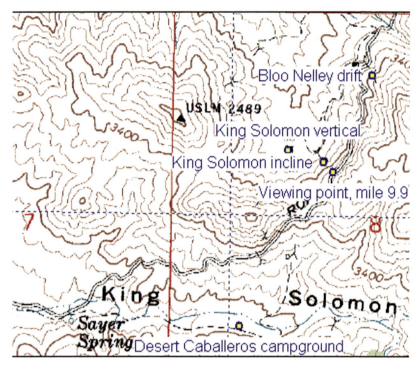

Unida Group

two primary veins of ore with a total of 1,760 feet of underground tunnels.

The King Solomon Vein has both an incline and a vertical shaft into the vein. This vein of ore actually extends from the south/southeast at the King Solomon Mine shaft, now occupied by the Owl Springs Ranch and located several miles away. At this time, look to your right at the cut in the hill made by the roadway. Can you identify the dark colored three to four foot vein of ore? This is the actual vein of copper ore. Remaining where you are, look over the edge. The incline shaft is directly below the road along the angle of this vein. It contained very good copper ore and some gold as well. It extends down only 285 feet and has a horizontal drift at the first level, 100 feet below the surface of the shaft and extending to the west out to the surface and further on to a tailing pile that you can see. Out to the left, in the middle of the area, you will see an obvious shaft area. This is a vertical shaft that

One of several stone houses in the Unida Group

never reached the main vein. It is 350 feet deep but did uncover a five foot wide spur of good ore.

In 1925 it was estimated there was some 400,000 tons of ore available or about $10,000,000 worth. From September to December of 1974, four diamond-core sample holes were drilled on the King Solomon vein. These core samples estimated approximately 100,000 tons of ore—far less than the 1925 estimate.

One of the "modern" buildings

The Bloo Nelley vein is found further along the road. As you depart down Constellation Road from your stop for the King Solomon Vein mines, look for the first right turn that takes you up a slight incline (mileage 10.2). Park your vehicle and walk up this road, which leads to the second drift exposure from the main shaft. The primary shaft is actually on top of the mountain. There are three drifts from the main shaft that follow the body of ore and exit the side of the mountain. These exposures were very convenient as the miners no longer had to lift the ore and waste rock to the top, but could instead send it sideways and dump the material as it exited. The lowest drift, and last to

King Solomon ore vein along Constellation Road

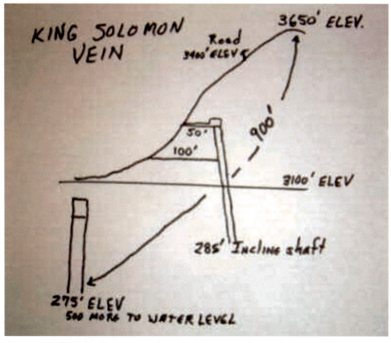
Unida Group—King Solomon vein underground
diagrams of both the incline and vertical shafts (Map at the Desert
Caballeros Western Museum, contributed by Dorothy Devault)

Unida Group—vertical shaft

be drilled, is 500 feet below the shaft at the top and extends 675 feet into the mountain side and to the vertical shaft. The second drift—the one you are stopped in front of—extends 550 feet into the mountain and has two vertical shafts within. This is a very dangerous place to be crawling around. The top drift, and first to see the light of day, extends 350 feet into the mountain to the primary vertical shaft.

The ore seams are said to vary in width from a mere seam to more than 12 feet with an average of three feet. The vein of ore extends over the mountain and in 1925 was estimated to contain 115,000 tons of ore.

A 1943 Field Engineer's Report showed very little record of ore shipments. There were some 50 tons in the tailing piles or "dumps" and most of these were processed during WWII. Some of this work was said to have been done by C.B. and Edmond Hays of Wickenburg.

From the available data at the Arizona Department of Mines and Mineral Resources, this entire area remains full of copper with good gold and some silver values as well.

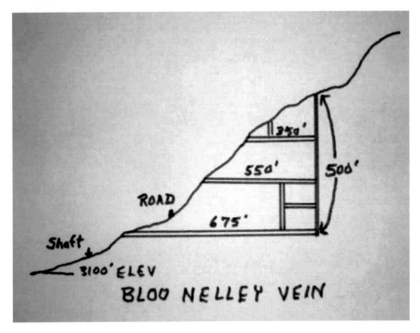

Unida Group—undergrounds at the Bloo Nelley (Map at the Desert Caballeros Western Museum, contributed by Dorothy Devault)

Mr. and Mrs. Jack Devault purchased this property in the early 1970s. Jack passed away in 1991 and Dorothy sold 187 acres of the property in early 2005.

As you drive on down the road, look left down Unida Wash where you could hike to the present day tallest saguaro (50'6", see *Desert Hiking Out Wickenburg Way*).

Unida Group—entrance to Bloo Nelley, second drift. Notice the old timbers and sluff-off of the rock/ore material. Stay out!

Chapter 4: The Monte Cristo

We now continue on toward the Monte Cristo Mine. About one mile ahead you will see a large dump of silver colored rock on your left (mileage 11.4). There is a deep exposed shaft here. It is a part of the Texas claims. We can't find the name or history even though it was a major digging. The "long lost power line" from the Octave Mine to Morgan's Butte came past this mine. We call it "long lost" as most of

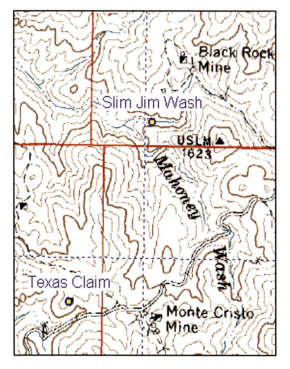

Monte Cristo and Black Rock

the poles have been cut and reused or rotted away, so the exact location is not clear. Moving forward, at the top of the grade a road goes off to the left; it drops into Slim Jim Wash. This washed-out road is to the Atos Mine, a major gold mine and the entrance to the wonderful "Balanced Rock Trail," which continues on to the Hassayampa River.

Dana at the Balanced Rock

There are many prospects in Slim Jim Wash as well as spectacular displays of desert flora and rock formations. Continue forward and you will see the head frame of the Monte Cristo Mine (mileage 11.6).

In the late 1800s, a small group of Mexican prospectors stumbled across an outcropping of rich silver ore. They built a kiln and only smelted the highest grade ores for several years. The kiln was a short distance down the gulch from their workings. Around it were tens of tons of slag, mute evidence of the large quantities of high-grade ore they had taken from their prospect holes and smelted.

Two claim jumpers forced them off at gunpoint, but the Mexicans had cunningly concealed the entrance to their mine. The claim jumpers looked and looked but could not find the actual mine. Having had a "grub stake" from a Phoenix hardware merchant, the claim jumpers were forced to release their find in payment for the grub stake to Ezra W. Thayer, a hardware merchant. Thayer and his workers also could not find the vein. As a result they hired Frank Crampton, author of the book *Deep Enough*, to find the entrance. On page 153 he states: "We were up at dawn and off to the Monte Cristo claims. We made a wide

Head frame at the Monte Cristo mine

detour around the camp so that the sound of our ponies hoofs would not be heard. We had been over the claims and almost all of the outcrops on foot, never on a pony, and everything looked different from the height of our saddles. We had not ridden a hundred yards along the outcrop that the Mexicans appeared to have worked on the most, when we discovered what we were looking for. ... The Mexicans had skillfully hidden the high grade seam by covering it with two-by-twelves and then throwing the worthless low-grade from the vein over them."

We think it interesting here to quote some other passages of *Deep Enough* as we believe it will give you a feel for how miners were treated and how tough the work really was. The following two paragraphs are from pages 154 and 155:

"Supper was over when we told Thayer where to look for his ore, but there was no waiting until morning; he wanted to determine whether we were right or wrong, or only guessing. The hard-rock stiffs were called out, sent into his shaft to drill short holes and, when that was done, to shoot them. When the powder smoke from the shots had cleared from the shaft, we went down. Some of the ladders were broken, skids for the incline-shaft bucket bashed up, and the hole an all around first-class mess with high-grade pieces, some as large as a corrugated wash-board, scattered through the mass of gob and low-grade ore from the main vein. Hanging from the roof were slabs, some as big as a door, of horn-silver, one of the richest of silver-ore minerals. One was removed later and used as a soft-toned bell.

"It took two weeks to take the high-grade from the roof of the shaft and at the same time timber to keep it from caving. When all the high-grade had been taken out, Thayer loaded it into two ore wagons to be hauled to Phoenix. Ed went with the lead wagon and John T in the other. Both were good six-gun men, and Thayer took no chances of theft of his silver ore. Thayer and his hard-rock stiffs went along on ponies as supplemental guardians while I remained to be handy in the unlikely event that Dilthey (an eastern speculator who had hired Crampton for some other work) showed up."

Thayer was very "set in his ways" and determined to open up a big mine. Instead of actually mining the ore, he spent over one-half million dollars in developing, or blocking out, the huge ore bodies. He often remarked that his money was safer in the ground than in a bank. According to the *Prescott Journal-Miner* at this time "assays from a 14-inch streak gave $4,000 per ton. According to the *Prescott Journal-Miner*, in February and April of 1915 they reported a work force of 20 to 30 men and a three-shift day.

From 1909 to 1921 the incline shaft was driven down 11 levels from 160 feet to over 1100 feet. There were over two miles of drifts and crosscuts disclosing thousands of tons of high-grade silver ore. They also reported finding large bodies of gold ore, one of them six feet in width. Again, according to the *Prescott Journal-Miner*, "Massive bodies of native silver are in evidence in all workings. Mining engineers are amazed at the marvelous mineral creation." Additionally, they reported: "at 960 feet there is a mineralogical change from white to red metal—and that the grade of the copper ore is exceptionally high." They reported three hoists or head frames on the properties, indicating

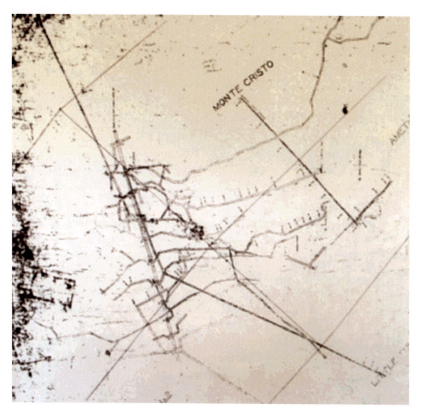

Undergrounds of the Monte Cristo mine

a total of three shafts connected by tunneling underground. We believe that one of these head frames was known as the Gold X.

In the meantime, various mining concerns approached Thayer with tempting offers. They were always met with a very definite "the Monte Cristo is NOT for sale;" that is, until 1926 when he could hold out no longer. We don't know why because in 1925 Mr. Thayer issued the following statement in *The Yavapai Magazine*:

"June 18, 1925

Monte Cristo Mining and Milling Co. Office, Phoenix, Arizona. Mines, Constellation, Arizona.

ASSETS:

38 Mining Claims—Approximately 700 acres. 800,000 shares of unissued stock. Gold, silver, copper. Engines, pumps, compressors, hoists, houses, tools, etc. Upward of twenty thousand feet of development, such as shafts, tunnels, levels, raises, crosscuts.

Working shaft eleven hundred feet deep, with levels run every hundred feet, each level connected with the other by raises, with crosscuts cutting parallel veins through both foot and hanging walls of great promise.

Many thousand tons of gold, copper and silver ores assaying from several dollars per ton to several thousand dollars per ton. Value, many millions, commercialized.

LIABILITIES

None.

Having bought from the sundry stockholders the issued stock, and believing the property had great merit, if properly developed and protected, I requested and obtained permission to be given a free hand in developing and advancing the company's interest at my own proper cost and expense.

I have expended several hundred thousand dollars of my own resources bringing the property to its present state of development, with no recourse or expectation other than expected by the minority stockholder.

It is with pride and pleasure I can say one need have no hesitancy in comparing our progress and acquisitions favorably with any.

Yours very truly,

EZRA W. THAYER"

In 1926 the Monte Cristo was sold to C.C. Julian of the Julian Merger Mines. Julian was a widely known promoter who purchased the mine for a reported $1 million in cash or half in cash and the other half in negotiable securities. Julian was apparently a shyster. He sold shares and also produced medallions. Julian never lifted a finger to mine any

Julian's medallions

ore and as a result both the medallions and shares were basically worthless.

Within two years a Phoenix rancher and previous minor stock holder brought suit against Julian alleging fraudulent intent on Julian's part. The rancher, A. Krell, asked for receivership and an injunction restraining defendants from further action with the company. To date (1928), the total receipts for ore and bullion were $14,531. In July of 1929, the mine sold at a sheriff's sale to A. Krell to satisfy a $9,449.45 judgment. From a million dollars to under ten thousand in only three years.

At this time there were 61 claims on 1200 acres with over 3½ miles of underground tunnels. There were also six other important veins on the property. Some of these claims were up the canyon while others were across the road and slightly closer to town. These were probably the Texas Claims.

Now the history gets really interesting. In 1933 the mine was sold to the Monte Cristo Gold Silver Co. of Utah. The sale was reported in the

Chapter 4 : The Monte Cristo

Monte Cristo stock certificate

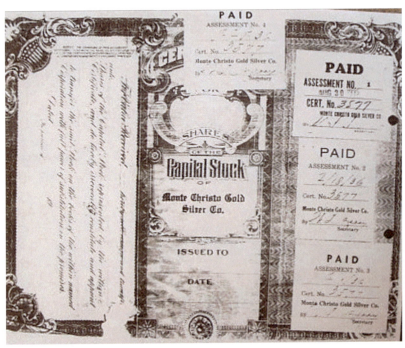

Back side of Monte Cristo stock certificate with assessment stamps

Prescott Journal-Miner, Feb. 14, 1933. They estimated a value of at least $5.6 million with the total value unknown but probably much more. This company put out a detailed prospectus glorifying the project and selling stock shares. Not only did they sell paper shares, they even levied assessments twice a year on this paper. While it was not stated in any readings we have found, they must have actually mined some materials because there is a cost basis for various jobs at the mine:

1. Freight rate to Wickenburg $3.75/ton
2. Freight rate to Hayden $4.00/ton (smelter location)
3. Miner $4.00/day
4. Mucker $3.25/day
5. Head millman $5.00/day
6. Hoistman $4.00/day
7. Blacksmith $4.50/day
8. Cook $50.00/month and board
9. Timberer $45.00/month and board

In 1945 "very strategic work" in conjunction with titanium and zirconium production was carried on at the Monte Cristo. As best the authors can find, neither of these materials are in the area. Another Julian?

In February of 1955 the International Ore Corporation unwatered the Monte Cristo and in 1956 the N.W. Development Corporation took over the mill and planned to reopen the mine.

In 1970 the wooden head frame and three buildings were burned—probably arson by juveniles seen leaving the area. The loss was reported at $25,000. By 1975 the current steel head frame was erected. It is said to have come from the Iron King mine near Dewey, AZ. In 1976 the Monte Cristo Mine was dewatered to the 800 foot level and it was found that most of the levels were caved in. They planned to bring

Monte Cristo—old wooden head-frame and
associated buildings from an old photo

in a mucking machine to reopen the tunnels; however, this did not happen.

In 1984 a W.K. Ramsey had a lease to purchase the mine and planned to dewater and reopen it. The Underdown family of Wickenburg also leased the claims but never did any real mining. The Underdowns held 32 claims until 2003 when they released their rights. A new claim has now been established over a portion of the old claims by an individual from Wittman, Arizona.

Ralph H. Speaker, a research engineer, wrote in 1940: "It is the writer's firm belief that, after the large bodies of gold and silver ores now proven and developed are mined, that, the development to further depth ... will prove the existence of a tremendous body of high grade copper ore. ... The Monte Cristo mine is absolutely virgin property and practically all of the ore developed and blocked out during the long period of development is still in the ground."

Who and what do you believe? This mine has certainly had an interesting and varied history, complete with fraudulent mining certificates and a lot of money lost by investors.

Chapter 5: The Black Rock

While standing at the Monte Cristo, look up the pass to the south. A trail to the pass connects with the Keystone Claims and the old original wagon road that connected to the town of Constellation. Little remains of the old road; it is now a popular horse and hiking trail. Dana thinks he drove the last jeep over that road in the 1960s.

As you stand at the Monte Cristo, look across the broad valley to the

Black Rock Mine—as seen across the wash from the Monte Cristo

north where you will see another mine tailing pile or dump across the wash (map, p. 27). This is the Black Rock Mine, also known as the Duluth-Arizona Mining Co. This mine was primarily a gold mine, with some silver and copper. Note the two very different colors in the dump. One is a very silver color similar to that found at the Monte

Cristo, the other is a much darker material, more associated with gold and copper.

The vertical shaft is 310 feet deep with three levels. The total development work was 1,147 feet of shafts, drifts and crosscuts. There are at least two stopes in the mine.

The investment in this mine was over $250,000 but the work was done without competent direction. In 1931 a J. T. Murphy of Duluth, Minnesota stated: "I was not personally interested in this property when the quarter million dollars was spent on it in a very crazy way by a bunch of spiritualists who had a meeting every Sunday night and asked the spirit to control what to do with their funds."

By 1935 however, the Duluth-Arizona Mining Co. planned to erect a 50-ton cyanide leaching plant. This did not take place and, unfortunately, we can find no more data on this property.

Chapter 6: More Sights Along the $17,000 Highway

Leaving the Monte Cristo, drive one-half mile over a ridge then drop into Slim Jim Wash (who was Slim Jim?) (mileage 12.2). Just before dropping in to the wash you will see a flat, open spot on your right. At one time this was said to be home to a Chinese Restaurant. It has also

Probable site of Chinese Restaurant above Slim Jim Wash

been rumored to be the home of a Post Office called "Constellation." On most any Arizona map you will find the town of Constellation annotated at this location. There is argument about the actual site of the town. In the early 1970s Dana was given photos of a mail wagon entering Constellation. He matched that photo to the terrain and found it at the windmill site one mile up Slim Jim Wash (map, p. vii). Those photos and many others were lost when the Desert Caballeros Western

Museum burned in 1973. It is possible that in later years with the advent of the new road, the Post Office was moved from the town site of Constellation to this spot along Slim Jim Wash. We simply don't know and have found no Post Office maps to confirm such a move.

In Slim Jim Wash you can travel downstream (left) by 4x4 a mile to Black Rock Mine. Be sure to leave the gate in the wash as you found it—open or closed. One of the neat aspects of this side trip is to see an ocotillo fence around what was the old main house. On the other side of Constellation Road and still in Slim Jim Wash, if you go right upstream one mile you will find the old town site of Constellation. On the way to Constellation you'll pass a cattle loading pen, a large mine and a road out to the left, which was the old way to O'Brien Wash and the Gold Bar Mine. At the old town site you will find many old rock

Constellation town site

foundations and some old broken bottle trash in several dumps. In his book *Deep Enough*, Frank Crampton writes and we paraphrase from page 142: "I found a town of a half-dozen buildings, the largest a two-

Old stage road entering Constellation town
site from the south, foundations on left and right

story stage station, a store, gambling den, and dance hall presided over by Powhattan S. Wren. Wren looked like a 5'3" Kentucky Colonel, even to the moustache and goatee. The only change was the addition of a Colt, which he displayed prominently while watching his poker tables and faro bank. He also rented rooms to girls from the Phoenix stockade, who came for a few weeks 'rest.' Local mining stiffs often visited Wren's home to see if the girls were getting the proper amount of 'rest.'"

Leaving Slim Jim Wash, the road starts uphill, through a cattle guard that separates the JV Bar and the Williams Ranch leases. Shortly past there is water tank supplied from a spring that comes out of an old mine. Continue up to the ridge where you can stop and savor the fabulous view of the backcountry of the Bradshaws (mileage 13.1). Look-

Cattle guard just above Slim Jim Wash and entrance to the Williams Ranch leases. Notice three different brands of the Williams Ranch on the left side.

Backcountry of the Bradshaw mountains

ing northwest in the Weaver Mountains you see Wades Butte (two small pinnacles); to the right is Seal Peak, depicted on the Arizona

Seal Peak

Territorial Seal. Note, the Hassayampa River splits the Weavers from the Bradshaws. Looking east you see Horse Mountain (steep rock cliffs), and Towers Mountain (named for Mr. Towers, but hosts many communication antenna and a fire tower at 8000 feet elevation in the tall pines). Right of Towers is the Crown King area and Horsethief Basin. This is fabulous high country for exploring; old mine remains are everywhere including the ghost towns of Bradshaw City (once talked of as state capital), Tiger and Oro Bello, Fort Misery, the Convict Road and more wild and wonderful country to explore.

Continue on Constellation Road where a fork to the left goes across the face of Mahoney Peak to the George Washington Mine and great hiking trail heads (mileage 13.2). Bear right and drop off the hillside from this beautiful view sight.

Intersection of the road to the George Washington Mine—keep right

Chapter 7: The Gold Bar

As you continue forward, you will make a few switchbacks and, on the left, see the relics of the Gold Bar Mine (mileage 13.6). There are additional prospects on the right side of the road; however, there is no data available on them. Most of the data on this mine were taken from David Twichell's "History of Gold Bar Mine and General Mining Observations." Very little data were found at the Arizona Department of Mines and Mineral Resources.

In 1877 James Mahoney made a discovery of gold. He did not register his claim until October of 1888. He then registered four claims of 20 acres each and later obtained one other claim between his four. His Glory Hole (original find location) was mined until 1902 (see diagram).

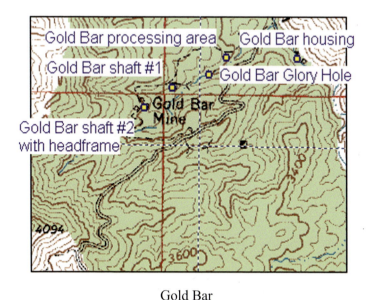

Gold Bar

By 1895, Mahoney sold half of his interest to Francis Xavier O'Brien, an experienced Colorado mining man. In 1899, O'Brien obtained the other half interest. Somehow, and unexplained, he ended up with eight claims.

O'Brien, in 1902, united with D.L. Murray, R.W. Baxter and F.L. Baldwin to form the Interior Mining and Trust Corporation. They could sell a maximum of $3 million in stock. The purchaser of an unknown, but probably large amount of stock, was J.A. Twichell. By this time they had sunk #1 shaft, eventually to 325 feet. From the cur-

Gold Bar—to right of head-frame #2. At top of tailing pile (dump) on left was head-frame #1

rent head frame at #2 look down to the right several hundred yards. You will see some old mining debris and a lone saguaro cactus. Just to the right of the cactus is a small fenced-in area that is the #1 shaft. To the right of it is the dump or tailing pile. This shaft is up hill from the Glory Hole, which is further down the valley to the right and not visible from the road at this point. From the bottom of the #1 shaft they had an incline adize (winch) into the Glory Hole and the underground was mined out into a large stope. Unlike the Monte Cristo, this mine was being developed and mined (ore removed and sold).

By 1907 the #2 shaft was begun. You can see the head frame associated with this vertical shaft. By 1917 this shaft reached a depth of 735

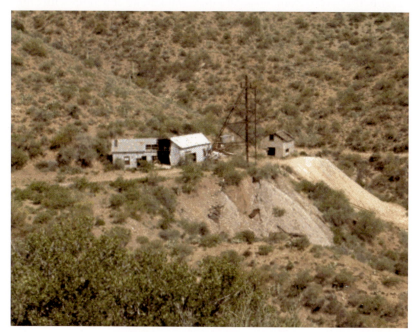

Gold Bar—head-frame of shaft #2

feet. A year earlier, it was connected underground to the #1 shaft. It took ten years of digging, probably not continuously, to get from the surface through waste rock to reach the gold formation at over 700 feet deep. They were now ready to begin mining the ore and developing stopes between #1 and #2 shafts.

Additional insight into this period comes from the *Prescott Journal-Miner* in 1917:

"ONCE AGAIN ON ACTIVE LIST

"Gold Bar Mines Company takes over and will operate Wickenburg property.

"The Gold Bar Mines Company has taken over the Interior Mining and Trust property, near Wickenburg, and started work on a large scale.

"The property acquired consists of 34 claims, located near Wickenburg and has a large mill equipped with 12 Nisson stamps of 100 tons

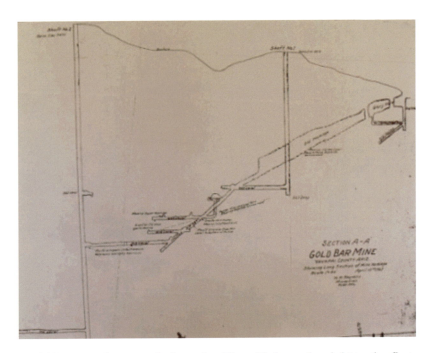

Gold Bar—undergrounds from the Glory Hole on the right to the first and second shafts on the left. Notice the huge stoped area between the Glory Hole and past the #1 shaft. (Map at the Desert Caballeros Western Museum, contributed by Dorothy Devault)

a day capacity, two Frue vanners and six Wilfley tables (see mining terminology). There is a 60-horsepower gasoline engine to run a mill with other engines for the hoist, tables, compressor and pump. There was also a company store, boarding house, club house and office buildings. An office building and store houses with platforms for handling freight occupy two tracts of land in Wickenburg. T.N. Jenks, a mining engineer of 23 years experience in the western mining country has been engaged as manager to look after the property and operations of the company, and is now in active service at the camp.

"The mine was formerly a producer for eight months, extending from October 1, 1907 to June 1, 1908. The gold bullion produced and sold by the company amounted to $95,762.63 at an average cost of $3.29 for mining and milling the ore. This gold was produced from the 325 foot level. In the summer of 1908 this working caved in completely and operations ceased until money was raised by a bond issue for the purpose of sinking a new shaft. This shaft, which is a twin-compartment shaft was sunk to a depth of 240 feet at a point conveniently near the old shaft. On account of exhausting the funds on hand from the bond issue, operations were abandoned at this point, but the office of the company now claims the company has raised sufficient money to finish the work.

"It is the intention of the company to finish sinking the shaft to a depth of 625 feet. The company proposes to tunnel across from the 325 foot level for the purpose of taking out the gold from the old workings, at the same time continuing sinking the shaft, as indications point to valuable copper deposits below the 325 foot level. There are now two veins which, it is believed, should come together before the depth of 625 feet is reached and they are hopeful of securing a rich copper vein here."

An early eight-stamp mill was remodeled and by 1916 they had the 12-stamp mill in place. Driving forward you will see this location (mileage 13.9). The ground floor of the stamp mill fed eight concentrating tables and 22 amalgamation plates. None of this equipment is left. Below that, ten steel tanks of different sizes stood. A few of these remain today to the right of the stamp mill area. These tanks were used for cyanide processing for gold and silver recovery. There was also a lime shed and farther down to the right an assay office.

On the hill behind the stamp mill are three large tanks. These were water storage tanks. Water for this operation had to be pumped from the Hassayampa River several miles away.

Drive downhill until you see a road to the left (mileage 14.0). Drive in and park. Walk down to the streambed and go upstream. Currently this area is not posted for no trespassing; if such signs appear, please respect them and do not enter. Here you will find the Glory Hole. Be very careful as you can see how the roof of the stope has been caving in. Over time the Glory Hole has filled in with sediment and the sides continue to slough off. Notice the column in the center. This was left in place to hold up the roof. Do NOT enter the Glory Hole. Notice the tunnel on the left of the wash—a diversion tunnel to carry the creek water past the Glory Hole, not into it. This spring (2005) the dirt above the diversion tunnel also sloughed off, leaving that tunnel half filled with sediment. The tunnel is actually at least six feet tall.

Gold Bar—processing area and water storage tanks
using water pumped from the Hassayampa River

In 1916 the mine employed some 90 men and they spent $200,000. During ten months they processed 20,000 tons of ore or about $275,000 at $13.75 per ton. The ore, however, was found in an iron oxide matrix making cyanide recovery difficult. In 1917 the mine closed and the company failed, apparently due to the technical difficulties of processing the iron oxide ore matrix. Apparently, no technical advice was sought for the problem.

From 1927 to 1995 a dozen engineering and geologist reports all agree on a large amount of mineable ore with depth. The mine was unwatered in 1927, 1929, and 1934 for some of these studies. During this time there was always a caretaker on site. It is postulated many of them high-graded (stole ore from the mine).

In 1964 the mine was again pumped by a Canadian firm. This firm tore down and destroyed many buildings, damaged the shaft, did not pro-

Steel tanks for cyanide leach process at the Gold Bar

Gold Bar—entrance to the Glory Hole

Chapter 7 : The Gold Bar

vide samples of their work and left. At this time, Ward Twichell's widow and son David own the property.

In 1972 the mine was sold to Mr. and Mrs. Jack Devault. He died in 1991 and Dorothy still resides in Wickenburg. She sold the 298 acre property in early 2005.

Chapter 8: End of the Line—The Williams Ranch

Continuing along Constellation Road you will find some of the old buildings associated with the Gold Bar Mine (mileage 13.5). Please

Gold Bar—old building to house miners

obey the "No Trespassing" signs. We are now in O'Brien Wash. Follow the wash to join with Amazon Wash (mileage 14.5). For adventurers with good 4x4s, cross Amazon, turn right through a gate, then immediate left onto an antique road that connected the lower Hassayampa with Wagoner and Crown King roads. It also goes into Castle Creek past the grave of Isaac Bradshaw.

Go left and you arrive at the Williams Ranch, trail head to the Hassayampa Canyon Wilderness (mileage 15.1) and end of the Constella-

Gold Bar—decaying adobe building once holding a school on the second level

Gold Bar—homestead for owners located in O'Brien Wash below the mine

Chapter 8 : End of the Line—The Williams Ranch

Amazon and O'Brien washes

Entrance to the Williams Family Ranch

Chapter 8 : End of the Line—The Williams Ranch

tion Road. This ranch is a wonderful "old time" guest ranch where you can stay in a stack-log bunk house complete with indoor plumbing. This is an experience right out of the "old west" and one you really don't want to miss. Even if you don't ride horseback, you can explore along the banks of the Hassayampa River. Besides, the home cooked meals are fantastic. Roy and Carrol Williams are wonderful folks who, if they know ahead of time, can set you up with a lunch before you complete your travel home. Because of the lack of cell phone service in this Hassayampa River valley, you need to plan ahead and contact them several days or more before you intend to be at the ranch. Contact them at: cell phone 928-308-0589, or go to williamsfamilyranch@direcway.com, the best way to make contact. Also, check out their web page at: www.williamsfamilyranch.com.

Postface

You have now completed your journey *Where The Past Lives—Constellation Road*. It's time to turn around and follow the same road back to Wickenburg.

As you make the return journey, imagine yourself living out here in the late 1800s. Think of the hardships of living, working in mines and driving teams of animals to move equipment and personnel. Now, as you drive up the hill past the Gold Bar, imagine yourself sitting on a wagon driving a team of mules either up or down this hillside.

As you top the hill, you will have absolutely spectacular views out across Wickenburg and to Aguila. How far can you see? In Slim Jim Wash look upstream and imagine the town of Constellation. In several different sources it was said to be as important a location as Wickenburg. There was nothing to go to Wickenburg for, as Constellation had everything Wickenburg did—minus about 12 miles on horseback or on foot.

As you pass the Monte Cristo Mine, think of this hillside on both sides of the road teaming with tent housing. What would it be like living here as a man or a woman? Wash day had to be a lot of work!

As you approach the Unida Group and cross Unida Wash, look left and see if you can find the rock footing for the windmill that used to pump water from a well in this location. Slightly further along you literally cross over the Bloo Nelley's lower drift; how many men and how much work did it take to complete all the shafts, drifts and crosscuts.

Constellation Road is replete with history—much of which we have not learned or reported. Much of it will never be known. Clearly, however, this is a place "Where The Past Lives."

Postface

Appendix: Rich Hill

In 1863, Paulino Weaver led the Abraham Peeples' party of men (ex-49ers from the gold fields of California) into central Arizona from the Yuma area. Paulino, born in Tennessee and one-half Cherokee Indian, had traveled the southwest with the mountain men and also led 49ers from Santa Fe to the California gold fields via Southern Arizona. He was familiar with the desert and had heard stories of the gold in Apacheria (central Arizona). In the spring of 1863 Abraham Peeples and two other men contracted Weaver to lead them into the interior. Their party was too small, so they picked up six other men, including Henry Wickenburg. The party started up the Colorado River to the Bill Williams River, then turned inland, eventually arriving at the base of what is now called Rich Hill and the mountain range named after Weaver.

Local legend says they picketed their remuda of animals below the mountain and sometime during the night the entire remuda got loose. Several of the mules wandered to the top of the mountain and the two Mexican vaqueros with the party were dispatched to collect them. The story never says whether they collected the animals; instead, they found one of the richest finds of free standing gold anywhere in the world. As they picked up rocks to throw at the animals, they realized the ground was covered with gold nuggets and found some $4,000 apiece before breakfast. That area on top became known as the "potato patch," named for the potato-size nuggets of gold. To the southeast is an area the Irish called "Caugh-Oir" or Cup of Gold. On just one acre, over one-half million dollars in gold was picked up or pried out. The account of the finding of gold on top of Rich Hill in the book *Tales of Arizona Territory* by Charles D. Lauer makes no mention of animals becoming loose; rather they simply state the best ground (gold) was on top of the mountain.

The streams on both the east and west sides of Rich Hill have long been panned for placer gold. At Stanton on the west, panning at Antelope Creek continues today.

Above Rich Hill to the north is a big, broad, beautiful valley named after Abraham Peeples, Peeples Valley.

During the research for this book, the authors visited with Laura and Jack Culp of Congress, Arizona. Both have had a long history with Rich Hill. In fact, Laura's great-great grandfather, William Asa Moore of Paradise Valley/Humboldt Valley Nevada, arrived and prospected Rich Hill in 1864. He was a freighter to Phoenix as well as a horseback carrier of mail to Kirkland. The latter was done as a favor. Can you imagine riding a horse or mule from today's Stanton to Kirkland as a "favor"? Of course, you also had to return. Folks really took care of each other in those days! Until late in the 1800s miners had claims that were administered by the miners' organization. The claims may only be a few feet up a creek or a long section along a mountain—it was what the organization decided. Interestingly, Mexicans normally only got a three to five foot claim along a stream bed. Anglos got a lot more.

In those days, the Yavapai Indians who survived in this area considered the mountain a Spiritual Mountain. There were rumbling noises and water that came from the mountain and the noises are still heard today.

Laura's grandfather was Asa Vere Moore, married to Roena who, along with prospecting Rich Hill, ran a grocery store above today's Stanton. They had a daughter named Francis who married Tom Warren. Tom and Francis had three children, Laura, Richard and Roena. Asa worked with Mr. Hayden, a mining man who died in 1927. He owned the claims on Rich Hill and Asa paid the taxes and was given the deeds in 1938. The mines were worked until WWII. Grandpa had a ball mill on the site of the homestead above today's Stanton.

At one point in time there were some 37 cabins on top. Today there are only the remains of four cabins. There are some 54 acres under claim known as, in part, the Standard, Buckeye, Buckeye extension, and Empire. Along these claims are the water tunnel, and the Mud Pipe. There is an incline shaft in the middle of the "potato patch" that goes down some 300 feet.

Please do not attempt to climb Rich Hill as it is private property.

Remains of a rock cabin on Rich Hill

Laura Culp had some interesting stories of the old prospectors she met as a child on top of the mountain. Most were of WWI time frame and had been gassed or were otherwise a bit "off." She especially remembers one of these old timers who would sit and talk with her endlessly until the evening came. At that point he would say, "Little girl, it is time you go home before the little green people come out." After that he would sit before his abode with rifle in hand awaiting the "little green people." Laura said the folks were great. As a child her parents never worried where she was or with whom she talked. She spent her days wandering the mountain, visiting with the men who worked the area.

The Culps sold their claims in the fall of 2005. Today, there are many areas of Rich Hill that are still being worked. Be sure you know whose property you are on before you get shot!

References

1. Arizona Department of Mines and Mineral Resources Archives, 1502 W. Washington, Phoenix, AZ 85007.

2. Lauer, Charles D., *Tales of Arizona Territory*, Arizona Golden West Publishers, 1990.

3. Crampton, Frank, *Deep Enough*, University of Oklahoma Press, Norman, Oklahoma, 1982. (Copyright by the University of Oklahoma Press)

4. Desert Caballeros Western Museum Archives, Wickenburg, Arizona 85390.

5. Speaker, Ralph H., Engineering Report, 1940, found in Ref. 1 archives.

6. Twichell, David, "History of Gold Bar Mine and General Mining Observations," March 18, 1996. Paper resident at Ref. 4.

7. Sharlott Hall reference files of old newspapers, 415 W. Gurley St., Prescott, AZ 86301.

References

Index

Symbols
$17,000 Highway 17–23

A
adit xiii
Amazon Wash 53, 55
Amethyst Hill 8
Arizona Copper and Gold Co., see United Mining Co.
Arizona Department of Mines and Mineral Resources 23, 45, 63
Arizona Historical Foundation v
Arizona Historical Society xi
Atos Mine 27

B
Baldwin, F. L. 46
Baxter, R. W. 46
Black Rock Mine 37–38
Black Rock Mining District 17
Bloo Nelley Mine 22
Blue Tank Road 5, 6
Blue Tank Wash 8
Bradshaw City 43
Bradshaw Mountains 1
Buckhorn Springs Road 11
Buckhorn Wash 9
Burden, Sophie 5

C
cage xiv
Calamity Wash 4
collar xiv
Constellation (town) 37, 39, 40
Constellation Park 2
Constellation Road map vii

Crampton, Frank 28, 41, 63
crosscut xiii
Culp, Laura and Jack 60
Culture Keeper v, xi

D
Dana Ridge 9, 10
Denver Hill 9
Desert Caballeros Western Museum vi, ix, xii, 39, 63
Devault, Jack 23
Devault, Jack and Dorothy 52
drift xiii
Duluth-Arizona Mining Co. 37, 38

G
George Washington Mine 43, 44
Glory Hole 46
Glory Hole Mine 45, 49, 51
Gold Bar Mine 17, 40, 45–52, 53, 57
Gold X 31

H
Hamlin Wash 9
Hassayampa Canyon Wilderness 53
Hays, C. B. and Edmond 23
headframe xiii
Horse Mountain 43

I
Interior Mining and Trust Co. 46, 47

J
Julian, C. C. 32
JV Bar Ranch 8, 9, 42

K
Keystone Claims 37
King Solomon Mine 20
King Solomon Wash 9, 13–14
Krell, A. 33

L
Lauer, Charles D. 59, 63
level xiii

M
Mahoney vi
Mahoney Peak 43
Mahoney Ridge vi
Mahoney, James 17, 45
map
    Constellation Road vii
    Gold Bar 45
    Monte Cristo 27
    Unida Group 20
mines
    Atos 27
    Black Rock 37–38
    George Washington 43, 44
    Glory Hole 45, 49, 51
    Gold Bar 17, 40, 45–52, 53, 57
    King Solomon 20
    Monte Cristo 27–36, 37, 46, 57
    Octave 27
    Unida Group 57
    White 13

Monte Cristo Mine 27–36, 37, 46, 57
Moore, Asa Vere 60
Moore, William Asa 60
Murphy, J. T. 38
Murray, D. L. 46

O
O'Brien Wash 40, 55
O'Brien, Francis Xavier 45
Octave Mine 27
Owl Springs Ranch 20

P
Peeples Valley 60
Peeples, Abraham 59
Pete's Windmill 7
Powder House Wash 1
Prince, William Floyd 61

R
Ramsey, W. K. 36
Remuda Guest Ranch 2
Rich Hill vi, 11, 12, 59–61
Rincon Ranch 8

S
saguaro, tallest 13
Sayers Station 9, 13–14
Sayersville 9
Seal Peak 43
shaft xiii
Sharlott Hall Museum 63
Skeleton Ridge 3
skip xiii
Slim Jim Wash 27, 28, 39, 40, 42, 57

Speaker, Ralph H. 36, 63
Stagecoach Road 1, 6, 7
Stanton 59
stope xiii

T
Thayer, Ezra W. 28, 32
Three Falls 4
Towers Mountain 43
Twichell, David 63
Twichell, J. A. 46

U
Unida Group 17–23, 57
Unida Wash 57
United Mining Co. 19

W
Wade's Butte 43
Weaver Mountains 1, 43
Weaver, Paulino 59
White Mine 13
Wickenburg Clean and Beautiful xi
Williams Family Ranch vi, 42, 53, 55
Williams, Roy and Carrol vi
Wren, Powhattan S. 41

Quick order form

Fax orders: 928-684-0019. Send this form.

Telephone orders: 928-684-0019

E-mail orders: stevenscasita@msn.com

Postal orders: 860 S Los Altos Dr., Wickenburg, AZ 83590

Please send _____ copies of *Where The Past Lives—Constellation Road*

Price: $20.00 each (Call for quantity discount)

Shipping and handling $4.00 for the first book, $1.50 each subsequent book sent to the same address.

Please send more information of:

Other books____ Speaking ____ Consulting____ Guide services____

Name: _____

Address: _____

City: _____ State: ___ Zip:_____

Telephone: ____ - ____ - _____

E-mail address: _____

Payment: Check (Pathfinder Publishing) or cash